Heartlifting

Blessings to

_____

May God's unfailing love be your comfort.
May His compassions fill your heart with life.

God Bless You,

_____

_____

date

· PSALM 119:76–77

heartlifters®

for the *hurting*

Surprising Stories,
Stirring Messages, and
Refreshing Scriptures
That Make the
Heart Soar

Bob Kelly
Messages by
Caron Loveless
Personalized Scriptures by
LeAnn Weiss

HOWARD
PUBLISHING CO.

Special foldout pages

Our purpose at Howard Publishing is to:

- *Increase faith* in the hearts of growing
  Christians
- *Inspire holiness* in the lives of believers
- *Instill hope* in the hearts of struggling people
  everywhere

Because He's coming again!

Heartlifters® for the Hurting © 2001 by Howard Publishing Company, Inc.
All rights reserved. Printed in Hong Kong
Published by Howard Publishing Co., Inc.
3117 North 7th Street, West Monroe, Louisiana 71291-2227

01 02 03 04 05 06 07 08 09 10   10 9 8 7 6 5 4 3 2 1

Personalized scriptures by LeAnn Weiss, owner of Encouragement Company
3006 Brandywine Dr., Orlando, FL 32806; (407) 898-4410

Edited by Philis Boultinghouse
Interior design by Lecy Design, Minneapolis, Minnesota

Library of Congress Cataloging-in-Publication Data
Kelly, Bob, 1929-
   Heartlifters for the hurting : surprising stories, stirring messages, and refreshing
  scriptures that make the heart soar / Bob Kelly ; messages by Caron Loveless ;
  personalized scriptures by LeAnn Weiss.
     p. cm.
  Includes bibliographical references.
  ISBN 1-58229-202-7
   1. Consolation. I. Loveless, Caron, 1955- II. Weiss, LeAnn. III. Title
BV4905.3 K44 2001
242'.4—dc21   2001024775

Contents

The purest ore is produced
from the hottest furnace,
and the brightest
thunderbolt is elicited
from the darkest storm.

—CHARLES CALEB COLTON

Overcoming THE DARKNESS

It had been an exciting weekend for Renée Lacouague. On Saturday evening Mike had given her a beautiful diamond engagement ring. Then they had chaperoned the prom at the high school where Renée taught music and directed the choir, jitterbugging the evening away.

The next night, May 16, 1988, after preparing the coming week's lesson plan, Renée went to bed, exhausted but excited about the future, which in two months would include her wedding day.

She awoke from a sound sleep to find herself diving off the foot of her bed. She lay dazed on the floor, unable to move, in excruciating pain. She tried calling Dorothy, who lived with her, but could barely whisper. *She'll never hear me,* she thought. But almost immediately, Dorothy opened her door.

Startled, Dorothy asked, "What are you doing on the floor? It's 2 A.M.!" Renée was in so much pain that she could barely reply. She awoke the next day in a hospital bed, where she learned she'd broken her neck and was paralyzed. "I'm afraid you'll never be able to walk, sit up, use your arms or legs, or sing again," the doctor said.

How could this be? One minute she was dancing and making wedding plans. The next, she was a quadriplegic—destined to spend the rest of her life in a wheelchair! It was unimaginable; she had no history of sleepwalking or seizures. Apparently, she'd dreamed she was diving—a dream so vivid that it became reality.

This can't really be happening, she thought as she lay there. *I went to bed happy and healthy. Now I'm helpless. There'll be no singing or teaching and no wedding. It's not fair to expect Mike to marry me now.*

At first, her faith in God kept her going. She was sure that her condition was temporary and that He would soon heal her. But as the months passed without any change, she became deeply frustrated and cried out to God to restore her body.

Gradually, her frustration turned to acceptance, and her faith grew stronger than ever. She began seeing the Lord's provision at every turn. Mike stayed beside her during her five months in the hospital, and a year after Renée's release, they were married.

Renée slowly regained some movement in her arms, and despite the prognosis, her beautiful singing voice returned. At her pastor's invitation, she began directing the church's youth choirs, grateful for the chance to be teaching again. But then, against seemingly impossible odds, she gave birth to a son. With singing and speaking requests coming in, she needed to relinquish her choir activities.

Now a popular singer and speaker, Renée tours the country, thrilling audiences with her beautiful singing voice, radiant smile, and testimony of God's grace in her life. She says, "Until recently, I couldn't see a clear purpose for my injury, but as I rolled out onto a stage to witness to ten thousand teenagers, it hit me like a bolt of lightning. With a big smile I thought, *Lord, You are so funny! You did it. I am teaching again, and the classroom is a lot bigger!* God continues to use my bizarre accident to open the eyes of others to His peace that passes all understanding. At that moment, I knew beyond the shadow of a doubt that God has been—and still is—at work in my life."

Renée Bondi has traveled a long way from her days of helplessness and hopelessness. A wife, mother, singer, recording artist, and public speaker, she's a living testimony of God's grace as she spends each day "being confident of this, that he who began a good work in you will carry it on to completion until the day of Christ Jesus" (Philippians 1:6).

Some animals are creatures of the night. They live it up when the sun goes down. We, on the other hand, were not created to function in darkness. Like lost campers on a cloudy night, darkness disorients us. We fear the worst. Rustling leaves become bears. Cracking twigs might be bobcats. Near panic, we think, If only I had a flash-light…no telling what's out there…how much longer till sunrise?

We were made to live in the light, yet in certain seasons our lives reflect anything but that. We all face dark days— sometimes a string of them. In times of loss or abandon-ment, we may become shrouded by grief. Our hearts bow under the load. Hope is lost, and we feel ourselves sink beyond rescue.

We have heard that God dwells in unapproachable light. He is Light, and in Him is no darkness at all. So how does God deal with our dark side?

He may have left clues in creation.

Think of a hyacinth bulb. All winter long it lies entombed in the chilly mud, until finally, just when we're ready to give up, a stem juts through the dirt, dispensing a rapturous smell. Flowers find fuel in the dark. They are a constant reminder that even the bleakest winter prepares in secret for spring and that a once-dormant heart can, with time, learn to feel pleasure again.

A child is formed in a womb void of light. Then at the

appointed time, when the mother can hardly go on, labor suddenly starts and her baby is born. The birth of a baby brings hope. It shows us that out of our innermost darkness, life will come if only we'll wait for God's timing.

Nighttime can be the most difficult time of day. But even the night has a bright side if we'll see it. Each evening the twilight conveys, "Time to lay down your troubles. Rest your worries. Rest on God. Sleep in faith-filled confidence that, though you don't see it now, the light of dawn is closer than you think."

You are chosen! I've called you out of darkness into My marvelous light! I send forth My truth and light to guide you to Me. You are My workmanship, created in Christ Jesus to do good works, which I've prepared in advance for you to do. Serve with the strength I provide, giving the praise to Me. Watch Me faithfully complete the good work I've started in you!

Thinking of you always,

Your Creator and Light

1 Peter 2:9; Psalm 43:3; Ephesians 2:10
1 Peter 4:11; Philippians 1:6

I've called you into My marvelous light...

Sorrows are often like clouds,
which though black when
they are passing over us,
when they are past become
as if they were the garments
of God thrown off in purple
and gold along the sky.

—HENRY WARD BEECHER

Victory over
DEPRESSION

Janice always seemed to have it all together until a series of tragedies began taking their toll. Her husband, David, a successful professional, had recently broken his arm, which was already weakened by cancer, threatening both his career and his life. Then a phone call brought news of the sudden death of her father at age sixty-four.

The pain she'd felt from another call seven years earlier came flooding back. Her husband, who was away, had called to tell her of her mother's sudden death.

This new blow hit her hard. "The pain that welled up inside me when my father died," she said, "included all the pain I had stuffed since my mother died."

It was the beginning of a long downhill slide for Jan. To block out the pain, she stayed busy and insisted she was fine. With a sick husband and two young children, she had too many responsibilities to worry about herself. But the tremendous stress began to wear her down. Heartburn and severe indigestion became daily occurrences. Then, without warning, she began having panic attacks. Finally, she sought help.

Thinking she had the flu, she went to a doctor, only to be shocked by his diagnosis—depression! Despite his explanation of how depression manifests itself both physiologically and psychologically, Jan was appalled. "It is not depression! I don't feel depressed. I'm a Christian, and Christians don't get depressed."

As her condition worsened, the doctor prescribed an antidepressant, which left her bedridden. Her inability to function brought tremendous guilt; so in desperation, she agreed to see a psychiatrist.

But things got worse. A pastor friend recommended a Christian counselor. But visits with him upset her, as did the words of disapproval from her pastor and Christian friends, who saw counseling as contrary to Scripture and unspiritual.

Still another doctor confirmed her depression and recommended antidepressant medication or counseling or both. But Jan decided, "I have had enough! I am going to bed. All I need—all I want—is some rest."

Then came more bad news. A new tumor had been discovered in Dave's arm, requiring more surgery. Afterward, the oncologist told them amputation would probably be the next step.

Jan had reached bottom. "I was experiencing moments of

utter darkness—dark days when I felt a black fog come over everything in my life. I had lost all joy."

As Dave's condition worsened, he finally agreed to amputation, which took place on June 18, 1991. Oddly, that act of surrender brought a sense of peace, not only to Dave but to Jan as well. "In a spiritual sense, I needed surgery, too, just as much as Dave did." She felt God saying, "Jan, your reliance on yourself is like trying to revive the flesh. Your own strength and goodness will never be sufficient for the life I want you to live."

Eventually, after extensive Christian counseling, Jan, too, was restored. In 1993, she and Dave launched their own ministry based in Colorado Springs, Colorado. Its purpose was to bring hope and

healing to those whose lives had been devastated by cancer and amputation—and by depression.

"My illness was as real as Dave's," Jan shares, "but the arm is visible, while the brain is not. Christians never need be ashamed to seek help for depression. Look in the psalms to discover the depression King David suffered. But God was faithful to him, as He has been to my own David and to me."

Fittingly, the ministry of Jan's husband, a former major-league pitcher whose career was cut short by cancer, is called Dave Dravecky's Outreach of Hope. Their message is beautifully told in Jan's book, *A Joy I'd Never Known*.

Take a step toward healing today. Just one. Do not get distracted with how long it might take to reach wholeness. Now is not the time to think about that. There is only time now to begin. Move yourself closer to joy by trying one of the following suggestions:

- *Take your dog for a walk—but follow a brand-new path. If you don't have a dog, borrow one from your neighbor.*

- *Read the biography of someone who triumphed in spite of great challenges. Read outside in the sunshine.*

- *Find the nearest body of water and drink in the view. Go fishing, skip rocks, and even if it's cold, take off your shoes and wade in.*

- *If you don't normally do this, read the comic section of the newspaper—twice. Cut out the best comic. Stick it on your refrigerator.*

- *Rent a video of the funniest movie you have ever seen.*

- *Buy two bunches of daisies. Distribute one bunch in vases throughout the main rooms of your house. Give the other bunch to the oldest woman on your block.*

- *Eat a Popsicle or an ice cream sandwich, recalling a pleasant time in your childhood.*

- *Ride a bike through a sprinkler.*

- *Phone a relative and do all the listening.*

- *Write in your journal. Express how you feel. Describe the highs as well as the lows. Write your heart out.*

- *Take a drive with the windows rolled down. Find an*

oldies station on the radio and sing along. How many songs can you remember word for word?

- Have a picnic in the park. Invite a child to join you. Take along bubbles and bread crumbs.

- Pray for three people in need. Pray out loud.

- Send a "thinking of you" card to someone you know needs encouragement.

- Go to church.

- Visit a support group you keep meaning to try.

- Read a chapter in the Bible. Psalms 16 and 20 are good ones.

- Tomorrow take one more step.

*Look up
and remember...*

The only way to meet affliction is to pass through it solemnly, slowly, with humility and faith, as the Israelites passed through the sea. Then its very waves of misery will divide, and become to us a wall, on the right side and on the left, until the gulf narrows before our eyes, and we land safe on the opposite shore.

—DINAH MARIA
    MULOCK CRAIK

The handsome basketball star and the pretty, vivacious cheerleader attended the same high school in Wilmington, Delaware. It seemed the perfect setting for a storybook romance, but for Lois and Jack, the romance had to wait. "He was the big man on campus," she says, "and barely ever looked in my direction."

They finally began dating after graduation and were married at age twenty-one. Jack was still in college, while Lois went off to work. After college, the young couple relocated to Fort Lauderdale, Florida. Their daughter Lisa was born in 1969, and Lara was born in 1972.

They were a close and happy family, active in their church and community.

Just before Christmas 1979, Lois surprised Jack by arranging a hot-air-balloon ride for him and his two close friends, Rick and Glenn. On the morning of December 15, the family excitedly headed off to join the other two men and their families.

As the balloon drifted across the sky, Lois and her daughters followed in their station wagon. They didn't see the gondola brush against some high-tension wires, but it was suddenly engulfed in flames. As the heat drove the balloon higher and higher, all three of the young men and their pilot leaped from the fiery basket to their deaths—in full view of their loved ones.

All three of these young men had a

strong Christian faith, as did the women they left behind. As thousands rushed to the scene of the tragedy, Lois and the other two wives, Gail and Kathy, shared the love of Christ with those who had come to render comfort to them.

Later, Lois told a reporter, "The event was very personal, but it was not private. Thousands of people knew about it within hours after it happened. And while death is always 'personal,' it's also an experience every individual must face someday. We shared what Christ did in this event so others can have the same assurance we have. We know our men are in heaven because they trusted Christ alone for their salvation…. Our purpose for still being in this world is to share the good news that Christ has defeated death."

Although the accident was spectacular in itself, it was this kind of reaction from the families that led to the making of a film about it. The film was a Gospel Films release called *Fire in the Sky*.

Lois moved to Colorado Springs in 1983 and remarried in 1989. Both Lisa and Lara are married and have presented their mother with seven grandchildren to date.

When asked to describe the grieving process, Lois replied, "It's different for everyone. Personality certainly plays a part. As an extrovert, I stayed active and busy. And a pastor friend gave me a mental picture that really helped me and the girls through our darkest times. Referring to Hebrews 11 and 12:1–2, he likened life to a race. He showed me that those who have completed the race are in heaven's grandstands, cheering for the ones still running. Since then, when I've been discouraged and weary, picturing this scene has helped me go on with renewed vision."

Lois has written several books including *The Snare, Daughters Without Dads,* and *When Your Soul Aches*; has been interviewed many times on radio and television; and has been a featured speaker at Billy Graham and Luis Palau crusades and at numerous other events. Today, more than twenty years after Jack's death, Lois Mowday Rabey, with husband, Steve Rabey, at her side, continues to run the race, sharing the good news of Christ and serving the Lord she loves.

During a time of loss or suffering, a special form of grace can rest on you. It is unexplainable in human terms. But with it you acquire a supernatural peace that transcends your circumstances.

To access this grace, pause where you are and begin to pour out your heart to God. Exchange your present feelings for His tranquillity. Nothing you say can offend God. He has heard it all. Nothing you think will disturb Him. Just speak to Him like a cherished friend and ask for a generous dose of the peace that passes all understanding.

As you lay your heart before God, expect to receive the unlimited resources of His kingdom. Take all you need.

God's compassion sits stored and waiting to be measured out at a moment's notice to anyone who asks.

God is your refuge, a tower of strength in your day of trouble. So run to Him. Give Him your confusion, and let Him comfort you as His child. Christ came to heal the brokenhearted. It gives Him joy to lift your spirit of heaviness with His healing oil of gladness.

Ask Him for the kind of grace that will enable you to stand firm when all your strength is gone. He gives freely and generously to all who ask for His help.

Position your heart to run toward the path of God's presence. Picture yourself seated with Christ in heavenly places each time the cares of your life overwhelm you. When you are tempted to take the weight of your heartache on your own shoulders, program yourself to pray. Day and night keep a running conversation with the Grace Giver. Hour by hour, give Him your hurt, fears, and loneliness.

With God comes a river of perfect peace that runs near your heart twenty-four hours a day. Reach up for it. Let it trickle down the cracks and soak the dry places in your soul.

Through every season of the soul, may God's grace and peace be yours in abundance.

You can
depend on Me...

The brightest crowns that
are worn in heaven have
been tried, and smelted,
and polished, and glorified
through the furnace
of affliction.

—EDWIN H. CHAPIN

"Fanny, pray to God to prepare you for all He is preparing for you." Those prophetic words from the dying mother she adored were to have a lifelong impact on the twelve-year-old child. Born in the early nineteenth century in England, she was the youngest of six children. Bright, high-spirited, and highly intelligent, she was nicknamed Little Quicksilver by her preacher father.

She was an avid reader, especially of poetry. To further her education, her father sent her off to boarding school in London, where strong religious teaching fortified what she had learned at home. At age fifteen, she wrote: "I committed my soul to the Saviour...and earth and heaven seemed bright from that moment."

Not long afterward, she suffered the first of what would be a lifelong series of serious illnesses and was sent home. A year later, her father and his new bride took Fanny with them to Germany. She became fluent in the language and eventually learned French, Italian, Greek, and Hebrew. To portray her merely as a sheltered intellectual and melancholy invalid, however, would be to paint an entirely false picture. When she was twenty, an older sister wrote about her, "Carolling like a bird she flashed into the room like a burst of sunshine.... With her sweet, fresh voice, she sang chants and hymns and played Handel."

From her father, Little Quicksilver had inherited a talent for music and became a skillful pianist, singer, and hymn writer. She described music as "a sort of alphabet of the language of heaven." Since childhood, she had enjoyed writing poetry, and her first volume of poems was published in 1869.

She remained strong in her faith, but her frequent illnesses brought periods of frustration and depression. At age thirty, during an illness, she wrote, "It has been very trying to me, this ill-health, very humbling to be a burden and a care, when I would rather have been a help and a lightener."

In 1871, at age thirty-five, she confessed to a friend, "I am stopped in every attempt at consecutive work.... Either ailments or something beyond my own control has always interfered ever since I was about twenty.... Pray for me, that I may really learn all He is teaching me."

Two years later, that prayer was answered. "On Advent

Sunday, December 2, 1873, I first saw clearly the blessedness of true consecration. I saw it as a flash of light, and what you see you can never unsee. There must be full surrender before there can be full blessedness…. It was made plain to me that He who had thus cleansed me had power to keep me clean; so I just utterly yielded myself to Him."

When illness struck again a few weeks later, she was able to say, "Two months ago this would have been a real trial to me…now *Thy will be done* is not a sigh but only a song!"

In the fall of 1875, she was stricken with typhoid fever and took nearly a year to recover, only to face a recurrence a short time later. In June 1879, an inflam-mation of her lungs ended her life prematurely at the age of forty-two.

Despite her relatively brief life, she left a rich legacy, which is still celebrated today. A prolific hymn writer, she wrote the lyrics of such great classics as *Who Is on the Lord's Side? Like a River Glorious,* and *Take My Life and Let It Be.* The words to that last-named hymn, written five years before her death, beautifully describe her own heart's desire. "Take my life and let it be consecrated, Lord, to Thee," was, indeed, the heart cry of Frances Ridley Havergal.

When you think you've lost sight of heaven, when all you feel is numbness where you once felt joy, then know it is time for a recount. It is time to recount all the ways you have seen God touch your life and remember some of the ways He has shown Himself faithful in Scripture.

Review the unforgettable deliverance God performed for the Hebrews in Egypt. Let the miracles that occurred there be a picture of how God can rescue you in the times you feel trapped or in bondage.

Think of the three young friends sentenced to death in a blazing furnace. Remember how they triumphantly survived, how their miracle turned a whole nation to God. You may never be thrown into a furnace, but their story gives assurance that God will be there with you no matter how hot things get.

Remember Job, the man who lost everything he ever loved or possessed. Even his health was attacked. Yet he still found that God could be trusted in spite of unbearable suffering. Ask God to give you Job's spirit.

Look back to the very beginning when God provided for Adam and Eve even after they sinned against Him.

Don't forget the brave mother who risked her own life to save the life of her baby, Moses, when she sent him down the Nile in a basket. Think how the child could have drowned but was rescued by the hand of God through

Pharaoh's daughter. Then recount a time when God used an unlikely person to rescue you.

Now think of Jesus. Remember the promise that He is the same yesterday, today, and forever. Know that no matter how desperate this season of life may be, you can fully trust your future to the God of Moses, Shadrach, and Job.

May the eyes of your heart open wide as you picture this ever-constant Jesus sitting on the right side of God in heaven. May you lean once again on the truth that day and night, every year of your life, He is seated there praying for you.

Today and every day, I send you special deliveries of My love and faithfulness. My love is better than life! I've made My light shine in your heart to give you the light of the knowledge of My glory in the face of Christ. Because of My great love for you, you are not destroyed. My compassions for you never fail; they are new and waiting for you each and every morning.

Loving you,

Your Faithful God

Psalms 57:3; 63:3; 2 Corinthians 4:6
Lamentations 3:22–23

My compassions never fail...

There is a sacredness in tears. They are not the mark of weakness, but of power. They speak more eloquently than 10,000 tongues. They are the messengers of overwhelming grief, of deep contrition and of unspeakable love.

—WASHINGTON IRVING

Discover blessings by putting your hope in Me. I am your helper! I save you when you're devastated, healing your broken heart and ministering to your deepest hurts. I comfort you through the darkest fear-filled valleys. I restore your mind, will, and emotions as I lead you to new heights. Over time, the silence of your heart and your tears will be transformed to treasures of joy.

Faithfully,

Your God Who Comforts You

Psalm 146:5–6; Hebrews 13:6
Psalms 34:18; 23:3–4; 30:11–12

Discover My blessings...

So much has been given
to me, I have no time to
ponder over that which has
been denied.

—HELEN KELLER

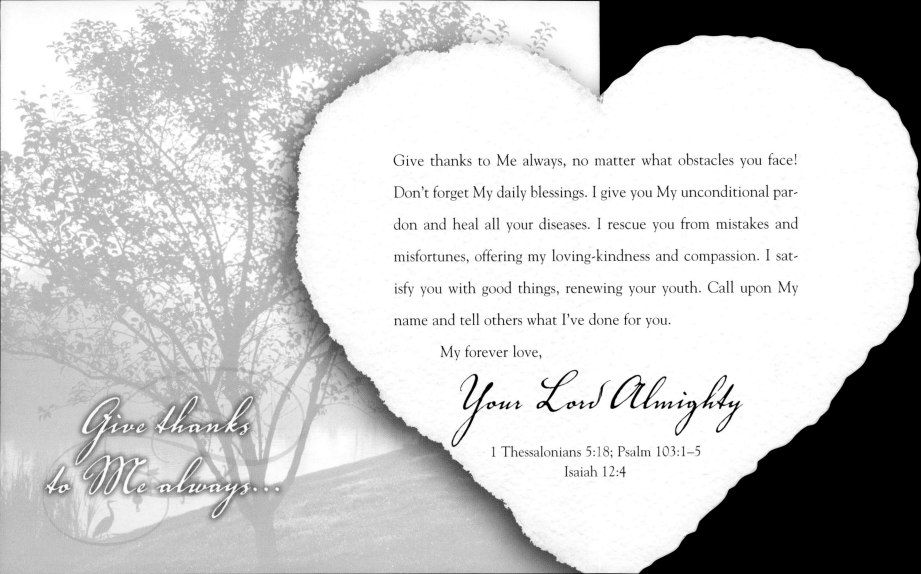

Give thanks to Me always, no matter what obstacles you face! Don't forget My daily blessings. I give you My unconditional pardon and heal all your diseases. I rescue you from mistakes and misfortunes, offering my loving-kindness and compassion. I satisfy you with good things, renewing your youth. Call upon My name and tell others what I've done for you.

My forever love,

Your Lord Almighty

1 Thessalonians 5:18; Psalm 103:1–5
Isaiah 12:4

Give thanks to Me always…

Mary and Jerry were in a Columbus, Ohio, hotel room when Jerry's secretary called with a message so tragic and unthinkable that it would change their lives forever. As Jerry listened to the voice of his secretary, his face grew instantly pale. Putting the phone aside and clasping his wife to him, he gently told her the terrible news: Their only son, Steve, had been murdered.

The previous night, a police officer had noticed bullet holes in the windshield of thirty-year-old Steve's taxicab and then had seen his bloodstained body behind the wheel.

In shock and disbelief, the grief-stricken parents made hurried arrangements to return to Colorado and to reach their three daughters with the terrible news before the media broke the story. Steve's wife, Julie, had been the first to receive the news. She'd been alone when police came and was reeling from shock and grief.

Steve had had his own radio show and drove a cab at night to help meet expenses. His family was concerned for his safety, but Steve would reassure them that he was careful to avoid threatening situations. Nevertheless, on that night in April 1990, someone had fired three bullets into the back of his head, killing him instantly.

The family all had strong Christian faith, but at times, the grief from the

sudden and terrible way Steve had been snatched from them became nearly unbearable. That first night Mary cried, "Did Steve see it coming? Was he threatened? Did he plead for his life? Did he call for me? Or Julie? Or his father? Oh, God, I should have been there. I'm his mother. He shouldn't have died alone like that, helpless, murdered, entombed in his cab. It's not fair. Please God, I can't bear this.... Help me to think of something else."

Each day brought fresh pain: an autopsy, funeral arrangements, viewing Steve's body, the burial and memorial service. Because of Jerry's leadership of a large international Christian organization, messages of love came in from all around the world. Unable to respond to each one personally, the family composed a long letter and sent copies to everyone.

In it, they asked, "How do you describe thirty years of life in a few pages? How do you communicate the sense of loss and grief we feel today? Words seem so inadequate. We are slowly coming to grips with the reality of his death. But daily

we are confronted with the 'nevers' of the future. Steve will never again walk in and say 'Hi, Mom, Hi, Dad.' He will never be the Santa Claus at Christmas gift openings around our tree.... The list is endless and painful, so what now? We must go on. Steve would have wanted it no differently. Although we miss him terribly, we know with a certainty that life does not end with death.... We focus our hope and confidence in God as we experience His help, comfort, and healing."

Today, Jerry White continues his work as president of The Navigators, an international ministry with a staff of 3,700 in 104 countries. Mary is an accomplished writer and a regular partner of her husband in ministry. Her book, *Harsh Grief, Gentle Hope*, telling the story of their son's death and of their own painful journey through the deepest valleys of grief, was published by NavPress in 1995.

In the final chapter, she wrote: "God was the one unchanging stability in my emotionally tilting universe. He knew my mourning; He knew just how severe my suffering was. He offered comfort and rest for my battered soul. In time, with His gentle help, healing came.... Truly, my soul and Jerry's were broken. But only the broken things of life need *restoration*, and that is what God offered us as we kept looking to Him for healing."

No one signs up for Valley duty. It is a season of the heart we avoid at all costs. But sooner or later we find ourselves there for different reasons and various lengths of time. Today, if you walk through The Valley, here are some thoughts for your passage.

Set your own pace. The Valley is a rugged, personal wilderness. Others may lag behind you; some will sprint ahead. Since this is your journey, travel at your own speed and with gear best suited for you.

Let others come to your aid. There will be days you can hardly set up camp and times when you walk with a limp. Fellow travelers will offer you shade and refreshment, places to rest your head or hang your heart. Take them.

Give thanks for them. Allow your soul every life-sip it can hold.

Drink. And eat. Eat even though you want to say, "What's the point? I have no appetite." These acts are your links to Reality. They will keep your mind from playing tricks the way a mind sometimes does to those passing through shadowlands.

Carry a songbook. You won't feel like singing. But sing anyway. Sing victory songs. Sing Valley songs. Sing to pass the night that drags like a wounded slug. Sing and then stop and listen. At first you might think you hear echoes or maybe an old mountaineer, but then suddenly you will recognize the sound.

It is Heaven's Voice come to sing with you.

Never mind that you do not know His songs. He has your song-book memorized. And don't be ashamed of your singing. He sings to the tune of your heart. Note for note, let His healing melodies mix with yours. Allow them to lift and carry you.

Soon your gait will quicken, and your stride will steady. The air will smell sweet. And you will be eager to move on.

That's when you turn and look back. Who knows how it happens?

Suddenly, finally, you will find yourself home on a hill far beyond The Valley.

Positively TREMENDOUS

Charles was five when his parents moved from Tallassee, Alabama, to Lancaster, Pennsylvania. The family was poor, but his jobless father, a boilermaker by trade, eventually found work building power plants in such distant places as the West Indies and Alaska.

Young Charles was never really a student. He got his first job at age twelve, starting each day at 4:00 A.M. By age fifteen, he'd had enough of school and found a job as a typist. At eighteen, he headed for Alaska, where his father worked in a power plant, and took a job breaking coal with a sledgehammer.

Four years later, back in Lancaster and selling men's furnishings, he met a young woman named Gloria. Thirteen weeks later, they were married.

Charles had returned to Alaska when news of Gloria's pregnancy brought him home for the birth of their first child. He briefly returned to his department store job but switched to life insurance sales in 1949.

Charles soon became an assistant manager, and by 1956, he was managing his own office. By 1965, he'd built an agency with more than 100 million dollars of life insurance in force.

Even though he achieved much success and prominence in the business world, the most significant event of his life had occurred in 1950. Charles had

attended church as a child and was later baptized, but he had never grasped the good news of the gospel—until a friend explained how he must place his trust in Christ alone for his eternal salvation.

Over the course of the next several years, his zeal for evangelism led him to leave his insurance business and become a public speaker, because this profession provided greater opportunities for evangelism than insurance. Then, in July 1999, a medical examination revealed the shocking news: cancer—advanced and inoperable!

What impact would the grave news have on this unique man who had laughed and hugged his way through life, spreading wit and wisdom, enthusiasm and exuberance, hilarity and hope, everywhere he went?

It didn't change him or slow him down, for even one minute. His periodic e-mails were filled with such phrases as "Thank God it's wonderful…. I wouldn't change a thing…. Lord willing, this will be a tremendous year in every way…. I'm feeling more uncomfortable talking about my condition

when I see how blessed I am…. I'm living in a wonderland."

As his cancer continued spreading, some friends wanted to honor him with a testimonial dinner. He agreed, on one condition—the testimonial would not be to him, but to the Lord Jesus Christ. And so, on September 1, 2000, Gloria, their six children, other family members, and more than five hundred of his closest friends gathered to celebrate his life. Prominently displayed everywhere were the words "Honoring the Lord Jesus Christ."

During the planning process, many of those involved visualized the event as a farewell tribute to their friend. But God had other ideas. In July 2000, a year after being diagnosed with cancer, Charles learned the disease had completely disappeared!

Over the years, millions of people have heard this world-renowned inspirational speaker tell his life story in fifteen seconds: "I'm not what I think I am; I'm not what I hoped I'd be; and I'm not what I ought to be. But by the grace of God, I'm not what I was. I once was lost, but now am found; was blind but now I see."

Recently named one of the top fifty speakers of the twentieth century, he's best known, not as Charles, but by the nickname "Tremendous," one he claims he received, not because of his accomplishments, but as the result of his own limited vocabulary: He repeatedly used the word in his speaking. But those who know him readily agree that it fits Charlie "Tremendous" Jones to a T.

What could seem more difficult than giving thanks when your heart aches? How do you learn to see past the natural realm and into a spiritual one? And why would an all-knowing, all-loving heavenly Father instruct His struggling child to be thankful regardless of the circumstances?

When we "give thanks in all things," we declare that we are focusing our energy on solutions rather than problems. It causes us to look to the Spirit rather than meditating on ourselves or a situation beyond our control. When we give thanks in all things, we are once again crowning Christ Lord over every area of our lives, and He in turn releases the power we need to withstand the storms that come against us.

A thankful heart is the secret weapon of the kingdom of

God. It is better able to resist the enemy and come against his attacks. A thankful heart boosts our God-confidence and reduces our fear.

The Scriptures invite us to come to the Lord with thanksgiving and enter His courts with praise. Because God dwells in the praises of His people, when we praise, we are never alone but are joined in a holy bond with Him. Praise keeps us connected to the Source of All Joy—even in times of great sorrow.

A thankful heart is in tune with the music of heaven. It is a harmonious heart—one that sees the flimsy, fleeting nature of this life and sets its sights on the prize far above it.

May God grant you the grace to speak words of thanks in

spite of mounting obstacles. May He give you strength to be grateful for all you have, even in times of great loss. At the very first sign of trouble, may you learn to quickly turn to the Savior, to thank Him for His might to overcome and His grace to endure. May this be a day when you practice the presence of God in all things. And when others show hurt or discouragement, may your thankful heart be the lifter of their heads.

The most beautiful mosaic is
but pieces of broken glass.
With divine aid, the scattered
fragments of our lives are
joined to make success.

—ELLA E. DODSON

Defeating DEFEAT

Augustine was born in Boston in 1923 to, in his words, "a tough little Irish mother" who dreamed he'd become a great writer. To nurture that dream, she had him reading adult books before he started kindergarten. During his high school days, they decided he would attend the School of Journalism at the University of Missouri.

In 1940, Augustine's mother dropped dead. *So much for dreams,* he thought, and he joined the U.S. Army Air Corps. After flying thirty World War II combat missions, he moved to New York, where he tried to find work, but "there wasn't a big demand for bombardiers with a high school education." Buying a used typewriter, he tried his hand at writing—without success.

Broke and discouraged, he returned to Boston, married his high school sweetheart, and began selling life insurance. After their daughter was born, they bought a small home. Determined to succeed, he worked long hours, later calling it "the most miserable ten years of my life." After work, he began stopping at a bar "for one drink," which soon became many. One night he got home to find that his wife and daughter had left him.

"Then I really hit bottom," he said. "I was a drunk, a thirty-five-year-old bum." After losing his house and his job, he roamed the country, taking any odd job he could find. "I was ready to end it all. I had thirty dollars left in my pocket, and when I saw a gun in a pawnshop for twenty-nine dollars, I almost bought it."

Instead, he went to a library and picked up a motivational book. "The writer," he said, "claimed you can be anything you want, with the help of God, if you're willing to pay the price." He contacted the author, who owned a business and hired him as a salesman. He did well, earning a promotion to sales manager. Taking a week off, he rented a typewriter and wrote a sales manual. "The dream," he said, "had never gone."

He was transferred to the company's headquarters in Chicago to write more manuals. When the editor of the motivational magazine that his company published retired, Augustine, encouraged by his new wife, asked for and was given the job.

With an empty space to fill in one of the issues, he wrote an article about Ben Hogan, who had come back from a near-fatal auto accident to win the U.S. Open Golf Championship. Months later, a New York publisher, sitting in his dentist's waiting room, read that article and was so impressed that he contacted Augustine, saying, "If you ever decide to write a book, get in touch with me." And so, in 1967, Augustine's first book was published.

Four years later, a major publisher, seeking the rights to a paperback edition, brought him to New York and offered him a lucrative contract. It was pouring rain when he left that office, so he ducked into the first open door he found. It was a small church, where he fell to his knees and began crying, thanking God for turning his life around. Then, looking up, he said,

"Hey, Mom, wherever you are, the kid made it!"

By the time of his death in 1996, the dream had more than come true. In all, Augustine had written eighteen books, which sold millions of copies in more than twenty languages, and had become one of the twentieth century's greatest inspirational writers and speakers. Along the way, he'd dropped his formal given name in favor of the nickname Og. The kid—Og Mandino—had indeed "made it!"

This may come as a surprise, but there are two letters of the alphabet that could change your life. These are modest letters, not the least bit flashy. You would hardly notice them at all if you passed them on the street. They couldn't form a word if they tried, but stick them in front of other words, and you have the potential for a dynamite situation.

Long before the rest of us (literally), God discovered these little letters. And sources say that of all the letters available to humankind, these two particular letters have turned out to be God's very own personal favorites. In fact, report has it that if you should ever see God driving down the highway, these same letters would be proudly displayed on his license plate.

However, some people do not feel that they deserve these letters. Many have not had life turn out as they planned. Mistakes have been made, or circumstances have prevented the degree of success they had hoped and sometimes prayed for. If you happen to be one of these people or know someone like that, it is time you learned what can happen with the help of re.

Re could start a revolution. With re you can get things back, try again, start anew. And at the front of certain words they create the potential (as we have said before, but it's well worth repeating) for a dynamite situation.

All the very best words start with re.

With re, you can take a broken heart, a broken dream, or

a broken vow and restore it. With re, a mangled marriage, a frantic father, or a moody mom can find recovery. But without re, faith could not be rekindled, love could not be reawakened, and hearts could not be reborn. Re increases the possibility that families will be reunited, values will be realigned, plans will be redirected, and that any person—no matter what they've done or where they've been—will receive a brand-new life when they put their trust in the Redeemer.

*My power
is perfected in
your weakness...*

See! The winter is past;

the rains are over and gone.

Flowers appear on the earth;

the season of singing

has come.

—SONG OF SONGS 2:11–12

Write your own story of how God has brought you comfort
and hope in your time of distress.

_____

_____

_____

_____

_____

_____

_____

_____

_____

_____

_____

Sources

Many sources were used in compiling the biographical sketches in this book. The following sources were primary.

Renée Bondi
Back On My Feet Again. San Juan Capistrano, Calif.: Capo Recording, 1998. Videocassette.
Telephone interviews with Renée Bondi.

Jan Dravecky
Jan Dravecky. *A Joy I'd Never Known.* Grand Rapids, Mich.: Zondervan Publishing House, 1996.
Telephone interviews with Jan Dravecky.

Lois Mowday Rabey
Telephone interviews with Lois Mowday Rabey.
Personal knowledge, based on long-term friendship with Lois Mowday Rabey.

Frances Ridley Havergal
T. H. Darlow. *Frances Ridley Havergal – A Saint of God.* London: Fleming Revell, 1927.

Sources

Mary & Jerry White
Mary A. White. *Harsh Grief, Gentle Hope*. Colorado Springs, Colo.: NavPress, 1995.
Telephone interviews with Jerry White.

Charlie "Tremendous" Jones
Personal and telephone interviews with Charlie Jones.
Personal knowledge, based on long-term friendship with Charlie Jones.

Og Mandino
Audiocassette of a workshop conducted by Og Mandino at the 1988 National Convention of the National Speakers Association, Phoenix, Ariz.

Other great gift books from Howard Publishing

Heartlifters Series:
Heartlifters for Mom
Heartlifters for Friends
Heartlifters for Women
Heartlifters for Hope and Joy
Heartlifters for Teachers
Heartlifters for the Young at Heart
Heartlifters for Sisters

Hugs Series:
Hugs for Teens
Hugs for Daughters
Hugs for Friends
Hugs for Dad
Hugs for Kids
Hugs for Mom
Hugs for Sisters
Hugs for Women
Hugs for Teachers
Hugs for Those in Love
Hugs for Grandparents
Hugs for the Holidays
Hugs for the Hurting
Hugs to Encourage and Inspire
Hugs for Grads
Hugs for Grandma

Hugs from Heaven Series:
Hugs from Heaven: Embraced by the Savior
Hugs from Heaven: On Angel Wings
Hugs from Heaven: The Christmas Story
Hugs from Heaven: Celebrating Friendship
Hugs from Heaven: Portraits of a Woman's Faith

Heavenly Mail Series:
Heavenly Mail: Words of Promise from God
Heavenly Mail: Words of Encouragement from God